The Stories of My Life

Books by Michael Schmidt include

Poetry
Collected Poems, smith|doorstop, 2009
The Resurrection of the Body, smith|doorstop, 2006
Selected Poems, smith|doorstop, 1997
The Love of Strangers, Century Hutchinson, 1989

Poetry Anthologies
New Poetries I-V, Carcanet, 1994-2011
Four American Poets, Carcanet, 2010
The Great Modern Poets, Quercus, 2007
The Harvill Book of Twentieth-Century Poetry in English, Harvill, 1999

Novels
The Dresden Gate, Century Hutchinson, 1988
The Colonist, Muller/Hutchinson, 1983

Translations
On Poets & Others, Octavio Paz, Paladin, 1991
Flower & Song: Nahuatl Poetry (with Edward Kissam), Anvil, 1977

Literary History and Criticism
A Life of the Novel, Harvard University Press, 2014
Lives of the Ancient Poets: The Greeks, Weidenfeld, 2004, Knopf, 2005
Lives of the Poets, Weidenfeld, 1998, Knopf, 1999
Reading Modern Poetry, Routledge, 1989
Fifty Modern British Poets: an introduction, Pan/Heinemann, 1979
Fifty English Poets 1300-1900: an introduction, Pan/Heinemann, 1979

Editions
Muriel Spark, *Mary Shelley*, Carcanet, 2013
Laura (Riding) Jackson, *The Telling*, Carcanet, 2005
Elizabeth Jennings, *Every Changing Shape*, Carcanet, 1996, 2002
Malcolm Lowry, *Under the Volcano*, Penguin, 2000

The Stories of My Life
Michael Schmidt

smith|doorstop

Published 2013 by
smith|doorstop Books
The Poetry Business
Bank Street Arts
32-40 Bank Street
Sheffield S1 2DS
www.poetrybusiness.co.uk

ISBN 978-1-906613-84-6

British Library Cataloguing-in-Publication Data.
A catalogue record for this book is available from the
British Library.

Typeset by Utter
Printed by printondemand.com
Cover design by Utter

smith|doorstop Books is a member of Inpress,
www.inpressbooks.co.uk. Distributed by Central Books Ltd.,
99 Wallis Road, London E9 5LN.

The Poetry Business is an Arts Council
National Portfolio Organisation

Supported by
**ARTS COUNCIL
ENGLAND**

for Ann & Peter Sansom

Acknowledgements

Versions of some of these poems appeared in *The First Poets* (Alfred A Knopf), *The Word Exchange* (W W Norton, 2010); *The Palm Beach Effect: Reflections on Michael Hofmann* (CB Editions, 2013); *Soul Feathers*, for Macmillan Cancer Support (2011); *Of Love and Hope*, a poetry anthology in aid of Breakthrough Breast Cancer and Breast Cancer Care (2010); and in *Oxford Magazine*, *PN Review*, *Poetry*, *Parnassus*, *Stand*, *The Reader* and *Tri-Quarterly*. The Greville Press pamphlet *Family Tree* was published in 2010, and for that I owe thanks to Anthony Astbury, one of poetry's champions. Four poems here were published in the 'new poems' section of my *Collected Poems* (2009).

'The Education of Henry Adams' was commissioned for *Lines in Long Array: A Civil War Commemoration* edited by David C Ward and Frank H Goodyear III and published by the Smithsonian, National Portrait Gallery, Washington D.C. (2013).

Contents

There was the Long Room, at one end of the garden, at the other the great gilded mirror, all blotches and dimples and ripples. I fluctuated in the watery glass; according to the light I retreated into the depths of the aquarium, or trembled in the foreground like a thread of pale-green samphire. Those who thought they knew me were ignorant of the creature I scarcely knew myself.

– Patrick White,
Flaws in the Glass: A Self-Portrait

But perhaps the time has come to give a name to the image appearing in the mirror's depth, which the painter in front of the picture contemplates.

– Michel Foucault,
'Las Meninas', part II, *Les mots et les choses*

I Les mots

Agatha

What is it like in heaven, Agatha?
I see you in those tight scuffed shoes, now dangling
Not over the playground wall (and your sharp knees
And the frayed serge skirt of your school uniform)
But off a black cloud hard against the blue.
They swing to and fro, to and fro, what can you see
So high above my head, and the tree and the hill?

Am I down here, is your house, is your lame cat Dorcas
With whiskers on the left side of her face
And a broken tail? Can you see us, do you want to now,
Recalled by the school alarm, the smell of asphalt
Softening in the sun, and the effulgent haze,
Or is all this fading, faded, faded out? If so, if your
Eyes have been able to uproot themselves from us,
Do they feed on the entire firmament, is it blue,
And is this as though it never had been at all,
Where I stand, where you used to sit on the wall?

What is it like, dear skinny Agatha,
With your sharp ribs under a stained singlet, your flat
Chest with nipples stuck on like round plasters,
Like valves, like coppers tipped slightly on smooth sand?
(We walked on the level shore at Capistrano
Gathering dark sand dollars and coolie-hat shells;
First we were five and six, then six and seven.)
What is it like, your straight lips pursed, your grey eyes, Agatha,
Gazing at a sky you're new in and new to?

And what is it like, dear Agatha, without me?
What colour is your hair now, how do you wear it?
Still in braids, or piled up high, in a bun or pony-tail?
I stand beneath your cloud and ask and ask.

Departure Lounge

In that child's I heard your childhood cry
Out again, a protracted yelling.
It made the woman carrying put
The dreadful bundle down and leave it
Squirming on the grass, and stand apart
Breathing deeply by the lake (the swans
Circling) watching the swans. The squirrels
Approach the squalling child and chuckle
Close by its swollen face, their brown eyes
Big, their tails pluming, three squirrels, then four
And your voice in that voice down all those
Years and lawns and lakes. Can I now reach
Your distress and take it in hand, hold
Close at my chest what you were, make some
Kind of peace?
                Delivering me red-eyed
At the airport at six this morning
You scalded your lips with a bitter
Costa coffee. Just before I left,
For the first time in years you broke, words
Sharp like your cries were back then. I should
Have stayed with you, whatever. My flight
Was called, we hugged. 'Back in a fortnight,'
I said and put the dreadful bundle
Down, in its need, in pain, by the lake,
Making my way helpless through customs
As she was then, as we are, fathers,
Mothers, when at last the child knows how
To speak his urgency, and we go.
The flight is called. I wave from the gate.

She Said

He went that way, quite fast, under the yellow tree
With a face red as a smacked behind, tears in his eyes,
Wearing again, she said, the moleskin trousers and tartan waistcoat
He wore to her wedding, the first, when the slut first said yes
Meaning the no it took her years to utter.

Oh, she remembered the waistcoat well enough, and she saw
How it became him despite the wake of years.
He was twenty-two again for a moment, she nineteen,
Her hair pulled back tight in a jet-black bun
And they stood there face to face with his hand on her breast.

How much she loved him still, how much she loved him!
It was easier to say no this second time,
Much easier, thanks to the practice she had had,
Thanks to the afternoon, and autumn, and he was old
And her heart had never healed so it didn't break again

When she felt his breath on her nape as he asked her.
That way, under the yellow tree, he went, she said,
In his tartan waistcoat, this time he was really gone
For good, she said, as though it mattered to her.

Feeding the Baby

             ...in the end
She fed her vampire everything she had,
Mother and father first, her husband
(In some ways she was glad to see him go);
Then the children one by one by one,
Keeping back, held close under her shawl,
Her favourite, in a milky gown, scowling,
Fat-handed, the pinkest mouthful of all.
When there was nothing left, she fed him
That one too, its salty fingers, china eyes,
Watched his slow jaw work a way right through it,
The baby shrilling a song as babies do
While it could, waving its bloody feet.
The vampire licked his chops and looked straight at her.

How much of her was his, was him by now,
Transformed to tissue, then to excrement,
And still he wasn't hers though she presumed
She'd earned herself a husband, he a wife.

She'd got no more to give. The vampire left her
One evening, not moonlit – 'just going to the shops'...

Carlisle to Kendal

A tumble of hills and then
that enchanted tower by
the river bend sensed even
in the dark, below Carlisle.

In the Woodcutter's Hut

In the woodcutter's hut the mattresses were stuffed
With beech-leaves and their scent. The drifting snow
Blacked out the window, sealed the door, we breathed
Thanks to the stone chimney. In fact,
It wasn't really cold, we had the cask,
Salt beef, the crate and loaves.
                                                    How the hours,
The hours slowed down, the nights, then the week also,
How they slowed
To breathing in the dark, the rise and fall,
And the pulse hardly ticking wrist and temple.

It seemed like days and days, we couldn't count,
We didn't talk in the dark, we didn't touch.
The beech trees told their season rosary,
From spring through autumn, over and over.
                                                    Cut
Before the sap was out of them, they stayed
Alive and in the blackout
We hibernated and were unafraid
Because the beech leaves kept telling their story
And when we dozed they lived again on our boughs,
In the good air we swayed, the beech leaves turning
First red, then green, then copper, and bright birds
Swam among them, perched, whetted their bills on our knuckles.
We were the beech boughs, tree skeletons, the gracious copse.
How long we slept! How they made use of us!
Without those mattresses we wouldn't have survived.
Now we're mast and nut and foliage, their bough, their tree.

Present Tense

The old man chews the air.
Under the ground his bride
Travels north and south
Transmitted by the worms,
Moles that scrabble through,
Maggot, vole and shrew.
When resurrection comes
Christ will have to raise
An entire field, she'll stand
On trunks for feet and pray
Like Laura turned to tree
With bough and bloom, her grey
Pupils made of dew,
Pulse a stammering breeze.

The old man senses her
And he is in her arms
Again, ago; both young
Exchange like ventricles,
Touch calling, answering touch,
Two climates, hemispheres,
Resolved in storm, in calm.

Under the chestnut's broad
Candled canopy
Clenched and comfortably
Alone he hugs his knees.
Among forget-me-not,
Bluebell and campion
He leans on a bending branch;
A smell of chamomile

Where his two feet are splayed
Rises from scuffed soil.

Then, into her dark leaves
Plump with the year, a flare,
A ring-dove: how she coos
Among the candles, light.
He listens to her voice,
Breathing the scented air.
Almost the scent is taste,
Almost the taste is touch.

His task is less than Christ's:
Her resurrection comes
To him as oxygen,
The voice, the chamomile;
She reaches like a hand
And closes on his heart.
A sweet time, this, to be
Alive and unalone,
Grace immaterial –
Reflection, not reflex.
He chews the given air.
It feeds him like a host.

Desire

Did we feel desire? We felt it. We felt desire.
And what did we do with it? We suffered it
Behind the ribs, between the eyes and the ears,
In bowel and groin, as if struggling for breath,
As if we had been tackled or felled or had fallen
Out of a normal day onto a fist.
Our own palms sweated and pricked,
We peered out between our fingers. It had not seen us.

What did we do next? We read it, we got it by heart;
We put our ears to it and heard its little lungs
Puffing. We kept it warm, we fed it sweet things,
We sang to it, we turned it on its bed,
Plumped its pillow, cleared away the pans.
We held it close, it smelled yeasty, it smelled of soil.
What did we do? For a year we harboured it,
As if we were a modest town by a bay

And it dropped anchor, furled its sails, ran up its pennants...
The beautiful sailors with their sharp starched blue flaps,
The captain a wingless angel... no, the captain a man,
And at night the Chinese lanterns, bobbing, enchanting,
An ensemble of pipes, tabors and a fiddle
Shuffling the heart, making it dance. It danced.
We watched from the quay and never went aboard.
They urged and urged us but we never went aboard.

One day it was all over. We woke, it had gone.
Like when the circus leaves a suburb lifeless,
Or it's Epiphany and all the lighted trees
Smoulder in back yards and the smoke makes tears.

We turned to one another then with nothing to hold
But one another. We stayed in the town by the bay.
A moon swelled out of the sea and, once risen, abated
Into a now literal night we inhabit together.

The Bus Stop

I missed the bus, and then it was of course
Too late to catch the train.
The rain came down through the shelter roof.
I sucked a cigarette and watched the rain.

I sucked a cigarette and tried to think
What, in the circumstances, I should do.
It was dark. There were lighted windows across the way,
Behind one of which, no doubt, were you,

Which is why I was in the cold and also why
I got there too late for the bus, and then for the train.
You kept me just long enough
So that I would have to come back to you again

Out of the dark, as if I was in love
Again, as if I could ever come back in love.

Answering the Emperor Julian
Mesopogon, after Cavafy

His face was ugly in a dozen ways. That's why
As soon as possible he grew the beard
To blur, to soften it. In time the 'shrubbery'
Concealed his hair lip and his crooked jaw,
And then the wiry throat, the pitted chest,
And combed out like an apron, grey and brown,
In middle age it hid the belly too,
Hid his desire, he combed and combed it.
Yet the face certainly was ugly still: the nose
Sunken, his left eye also. Ugly – but, in a sense,
No matter. He was different, he could not despise
The pauper, the halt, the leper and the man
Whose heart was broken on the horn of love.
(His heart was broken on the horn of love.)
Though he was emperor, he knew what it was like
To be subjected, knew what it could mean
To have your suppliants laughing in their sleeves
And not to be the god of your own temple.
Though they bowed down before him, touched the ground,
The rich, the poor, as his procession passed,
Once out of sight they sneered and blew their lips
Because of his nose and eyes, and more because
He wore that vast ridiculous coarse beard. Also
Because, unlike their previous kings, he knew them.

Triangulation

St John's and Reykjavik, St John's and Shannon:
A blue triangle, see it fill with shoals,
Some whales, the floes of ice, and seven ships,
Sea birds, honeycombs of sunlight, then
Dark in pie segments assembling a vast
Night, and from the north a giant disc of moon
Anarchic, starts to rise
Out of the mountain where hermits kneel
Statue-like, all bowed before
A queen's great absence now become white light.

II Les choses

Towards Monte Alban

High on the hill shanties catch
The day's first rays, not hot at all,
That dazzle, the ignition
Of white things, blades of glass, of tin
And clothes hung out (the poor are
The cleanest people, always). Eyes
Open pearl white, the iris
Sapphire. Eyes open pearl white on
The day's one good minute.
                       Sun
Goes downhill after that to a
Descending chorus of cocks.
Caws, little birds jump from their nests.
The near hills shift to distance.
What is close and is not clean and
Cannot dazzle clarifies.
Light dulls to haze. It's eight o'clock,
The shrill knife grinder rides by.
Heads down, the cocks are plucking dust.

Homage to Dr Atl

*Gerardo Murillo (1875-1964), pictor, depicter of
Iztaccíhuatl and Popocatépetl*

Was it really so lurid, so anarchic,
Dr Atl? Your palette persuaded you.
Those macaw-shrill floes, eruptions, impastos:
Apocalypse, then a primeval sunrise;
Geological eviscerations, ooze,
Blooms; among tuffa, obsidian blades: that's what
You saw, and your own eyes deeper, bloodshot, year
By year. Enormous canvases. If only
You could have scaled them up to the horizon!
What did you prop them against or fix them to
As you splattered them with vision?
                                    Made blind by
'That mountain Medusa' with his tangle beard
Who hopped on one leg, crag to crag, I soon fled
(As soon as it was decent) the 'Retrospect'
At the Muséo de Arte Moderno.
It was the long night of the 1960s.
I stumbled through the dark and off the pathways
Bathing my eyes clear in the garden fountains
And the sweet shadows of Chapultepec. How
Moderno were you, nineteenth-century, impure
Romantic of a world free of men, amen.

Yet the mountains were bodies you made love to.
Eros of pigment, Gerardo, how you slept
With them, on them, like Donne's am'rous flea fastened
To their skirts, their skin, your tiny bivouacs,
The wandering flare of your nightly campfires,
Corn cakes, tubs of bitter coffee, pots of broth;

Winged canvases dried by the fire's play of heat
And shadow, and you slept, your mouth to the rock,
Your little heart drumming the mountain's giant
Breast, *let me in, let me in*, and it let you
Lie there in the scrub with your lips on its heart.

Can a simple century have so rendered down
To monochrome? Today, certainly, flying
Over your habitat, your landscapes' contours
Drawn steeply up by the sun falling, haze is
All the residual bloom the mountains have,
And slow tumble of fumes from the crater's mouth
Downhill, dilating sulphur into a smog
Of the poisons of a world of men, amen.

The Education of Henry Adams, Private Secretary

Mansfield Street, Portland Place, London
– Towards a Cento

i.

Once only he saw Mr. Lincoln.
Washington, midnight, at winter's end,
A melancholy Inaugural.
Waltzes off-key, spurs, spittoons, and him
A long plain figure among those gowns:
Ploughed face, an air funereal in part
Due to a habit of foreboding,
In part to his too tight beige kid gloves.
No man in the Republic required
(He grimaced, saying it of himself)
More instruction than the President.

Lincoln, Seward, Sumner could not help
The greenhorn Private Secretary
With his slow *Education*; why, *they*
Knew as little as he did! (All through
The memoir his 'I' is 'he'.) He'd read
Six long years of Law; they'd practiced it
And what they did would cost ten thousand
Million dollars and a million lives.

On April thirteen Fort Sumter fell,
The storm burst, its lightning and thunder
Rolling several hundred thousand young
Men and Henry Adams in the surf
Of a wild ocean, all helpless like

Himself but not all safe. He had time
To go observe the regiments form
Ranks by the Boston State House, gather
In the solemn April evening and
Start the march south, with the docile frowns
They'd practiced to perfection from birth.
No drums and fifes, no kind of fanfare.
He had time to go down afterwards
To the port and embrace his brother
Charles, safe-quartered for the time being
In Fort Independence, the Army
Of the Republic falling into
Line around him, boots, belts and weapons,
In resolute blue rows, their numbers
Called. Nothing was so trivial that night
As the Private Secretary in
The dark, crawling down to the Cunard
Steamboat *Niagara* to sail again
With his father the Minister for
England.

     ii.

    In London Secretary
Adams carried messages, took tea,
Dictation, copied and recopied
Letters, betweentimes inching through Law,
Through Blackstone, like a termite through oak.
He suffered waking nightmares. The old
Duchess Dowager of Somerset,
A harridan with castanets, forced
The Turkish Ambassador's daughter
To perform a Highland fling with him.

The gentry smirked, clapped, and stamped their feet.
That night his pride came home in ashes.
He took for granted that his business
Was obedience, discipline, silence.
He never labored so hard to learn
A language as he did to hold his
Tongue, and it affected him for life.
A habit of reticence – talking
Without meaning – cannot be broken.

In his loneliness, when the story
Of Bull Run appeared in *The Times*, he
Hugged himself tight, felt a pang so deep,
Of his own absence from the one real
Story, that he was sick for a week.
He kept the door bolted. To be dead
With – no one knew the final number.
To be dead! And, breathing, he was dead.
Bull Run. The cause was lost. The English
Predicted history the moment
They recognized the South. Quite soon
They'd draw the line, do the final sums.
Events happened over there, the charge,
Retreat, flags in the mud, the bodies
Heaped, the carts and mules. But history
Happens at a distance, happens here
Where blood dries to ink. Minutiae,
Passions, amputations, don't survive
The transit from pain to history.
The subject burns down with the houses,
The soft goods, clocks and shifts, the bird cage.
Chimneys survive, memorializing –
One, two, three, four, five – the avenue.

What might have happened if he hadn't
Taken his father's counsel and flown
The coop, a Private Secretary?
Instead like men in uniform, in
Flames, alive or dead, and not a scribe
Reading the consequences of what
Should have been his story inscribed by
Thucydides.

iii.

                    Two years on, July,
In Pennsylvania. The bell's not chimed.
The rail fence holds, summer fields, the woods
Stand hospitable. The patient blue
And gray brigades find the countryside
Foreign as Palestine or Britain.
They stand to, tense, flags tight furled, breeze still.
It has not happened yet. If I don't
Put pen to paper, need it happen?
The Private Secretary dries the
Nib. Primed, on the mantle shelf the clock
Whirs, the English air waits for eight chimes.
(The voice of Longstreet rises in his
Throat, Kemper is sallow, grave Wilcox
Feels his heart dive like a fish. A jet
Of shrill sunlight bursts from Pickett's sword.)

The Private Secretary survives
A dream of bayonets. He lies stiff.
Time to go home, father, time to go.
Which his father answers with a stare
Open and empty.

Whitman wrote how
In some cemeteries north and south
Nearly all the dead are Unknown. At
Salisbury, North Carolina, the
Known are only eighty five, the un-
Known twelve thousand and twenty seven.
Eleven thousand seven hundred
Of these are buried in the furrows
The war ploughed in Lincoln's patient brow.

       iv.

Many a shock was Henry Adams
To meet in the course of a long life
Spent with politicians, politics.
The profoundest lessons are not those
Of reason: they're sudden strains that warp
The mind for good. It's a dismal school
Because the lessons never finish,
The war continues as the plough turns
Up in the fields new skulls, evidence
That numbers change. No name gets added.

Sherman's Georgia

i.

No one will tell the story straight.
What's there to tell it with but words?
They, too, are ruined, like the row
Of chimneys, hearths and fireplaces
Poking out of a mess of thorns
And evergreen. By the jetty
Where the trees are lame, they lean to
One another. Moss beards extend,
Floating on green water. Weeds and
Water weeds stink, high on summer.

ii.

I lean an elbow on a mantle shelf
Warmed by sun. In the old days it was fire.
Looking through a room my great grandfather
Looked into, and knocked his pipe, and squatted
To prod the coals, I see a space furnished
With hairy rattleweed full of spiders,
Coneflowers, quillwort, dropwort, the sumacs,
Stunted rue and campion, pungent nutmeg,
Confederate wakerobin, a silktree
Feathering, love in a puff, nut-sedge and
Lilacbell, cocklebur that killed the cows off,
the purple, velvet or the sandy sedge.

It's 1963, July the first,
Striking two o'clock. I find evidence:
Still a house of sorts, my great grandfather's

Property, tumbled walls, the shapes of rooms,
Doorsteps, stone outlasted the wood, withstood
The flames that took the avenue. The wood
And cotton burned, and all the rest of it.
No one tells the story. 2012.
The land's been cleared, the step swept clean away.

The Stories of My Life

i. Marginalia

By candle-light, the wavering text.
The pen he drives above the words
A wing in flight, its urgent pulse
In dialogue with what he reads
(As ventricle with ventricle
Exchanges confidence and blood,
Telltale and intimate, profane),
Its nib a beak, its nib a noise
Of rookeries, of pinions.
Out of the crystal pool it drinks,
Its voice is black... His lips make shapes
Of sound, his tongue tip like a kiss.

He frowns and notes, 'In getting books
I always seek a margin wide
As possible,' and this is for
'Comments, agreements, differences.'
If there's too little space he puts
'A slip of paper between leaves
Secured by imperceptible
Portions of gum tragacanth paste.'

He talks in whispers to himself,
'Freshly, boldly, without conceit.'
That's how his 'cynosures' communed
With God and Nature in old times,
Taylor, Temple, Thomas Browne,
'The anatomical Burton,
And Butler, that most logical

Analogist'. Their styles possessed
'A richly marginalic air.'

From these alert, immediate flights
His essays grow, his tales arise
Like Pandemonium from the dark
Exhaled, and Lucifer close by.
Into a text he plummets, soars,
And moonless rides its hurling waves;
Returning, perches on a plinth
And croaks his chilling negatives.

'Cover your nose,' says Henry James.
Poe is provincial, sulphurous,
Employing 'vitriol for ink',
'And yet...' So the concessions start.

Reading the tidy notes and runs
Precisely penned, as if a scribe
From Gower's stone scriptorium
Had travelled centuries to scratch
The tiny clarities, and sow
The seeds of stories, essays, poems,
The sense comes of a man enslaved
By that 'new nation' (not so new):
What might it say if moral terms
Took a fresh turn? The frayed homespun,
The bold primeval, street satire,
And patriotic garbage too
Were effortful and treacherous.
What might inherence give rise to?

In his cold flickering studio
Visit his windows on the night,

Frames with their inked out canvases
Emitting melodies, not sense;
Pain, pleasure no analysis
Can circumscribe or make disclose
In paraphrase a prose idea.
He stayed poor. His wife was dying.
He stayed poor and she died, a girl
He loved. His poems envisaged death.
It came, it went. No Orpheus,
And nothing said and nothing meant
And nothing say and nothing mean
Except the spell you cast and what
A spell can conjure out of naught.

ii. *'I love all men who dive.'*

'At nightfall Nantucket natives, out of sight
Of land, furl their sails, and lay them to their rest,
While under their very pillows rush the herds
Of walruses and whales.' That's where he started.

In 1849 he wrote to Duyckinck:
'I have been passing my time pleasurably,
Chiefly in lounging on a sofa (a la
The poet Grey) & reading Shakespeare, the book
In glorious great type, every letter whereof
Is a soldier, & the top of every "T"
Like a musket barrel.' At day school, textbooks
Had been the squinting, crammed and cheap editions
Printed to make verse mind-numbing for 'scholars',
Preparing them for the calculable worlds
Of lumber, harvest, bullion, prayer, timepieces,
Addition, and addition, profit, power.

Poetry, needlework, pianoforte
Were things girls did, refinements, added polish.
When it came to books, he was like other boys.
'My eyes were tender as young sparrows.' But now
On the gangway of the *Pequod*, as it were,
He 'chanced to fall in with this edition, I
Exult in it, page after page'.

                        Two years on,
To Duyckinck too, he told a happy story.
'I rise at eight – thereabouts – go to my barn –
Say good-morning to the horse, & give him his
Breakfast, pay a visit to my cow. – After,
I go to my work-room & light my fire – then
Spread my manuscript on the table – take one
Business squint at it, & fall to with a will.'
Five hours on the high seas, and then a knock,
He feeds the animals, dines, then rigs the sleigh,
Starts for the village, with mother or sisters.
'Evenings, in my room, unable to read, I
Spend in a mesmeric state, skimming over
Some large-printed book.' There was Shakespeare again,
His Virgil, pouring him through Hell's dark funnel.

More years: the inkwell dry, the page dry, his eyes
Sting. *Pequod*, Queequeg and his faith are all drowned.
The sharks, so fierce before, are now unharming,
'With padlocks on their mouths'; the silent sea-hawks
'Sail with sheathed beaks'. And last, the good ship *Rachel*
Misses her bobbing child and sets with the moon.

Not to Duyckinck now, with just his lips moving
He tells himself, 'You have not spared Ishmael.
You know what you have done and know how it's true,
You know the Saviour perished, but not for him.'

Thumbing the manuscript. 'This. Your book of ends.
You are exhausted with thrashing up and down
The watery paragraphs, now your hour's come.
But things don't finish as they ought, that's the way
The Fall refashioned the world, we each hang from
A cross we make for ourself; we drive the spikes
With an oak mallet into our palms and wrists,
Into our shins, right there above the heel-bone,
On some companionless Calvary, some whale-
Humped hill without the thieves or the three Maries,
Only the spear, sharp as a humming-bird's beak
Finding the heart's rose; and, rising to the lips
Like a kiss, a kiss, the sponge of vinegar.'

So he could tell the story at all, he must
Distort the truth, turn the good ship Rachel back
To hear the call (a necessary conceit,
As though the voice of a chosen child survived
The waves of flame in Ahab's pitch Gehenna),
'I'm Ishmael, survivor of the Pequod.
I am Jonah, survivor of the white whale.'

   iii. Hearsay

And Whitman? You never read his *Leaves*?
'But they told me he was disgraceful.'
Disgraceful? Now consider yourself!
Your life first offered on convention's
Happy altar, then snatched meanly back.
Your book too, like his, is appalling,
Miasmic, it changes with each reading,
Etching the living bone with diamond.

Your life was uneventful only
In the sense that no events attach
The vivid crises of your poems.
You lived out the War Between the States:
Rumors, the declaration, tolling,
Men mustered, parading in your street,
The tearful ritual of departure...
You stood, shadow, in the open door.
Then the wounded came home, and the dead
In boxes, as ghosts, or not at all.
Missing, you waited for the missing,
For twenty years, patiently, after
The war was done, in your snowy dress,
In your anxious room, as a widow
Knows what cannot be and yet it is:
Feel his breath, a light kiss on the nape.

Or you wait for Christ. Never a first
Communion, it's unction you wait for.
If only your knees would bend! Autumn
Buried by solving snow. No spring.
Saint Teresa knew what you learned, too:
In the particulars of this world
Only, if at all, can His wounds, His
Love be inferred, the transcendent *Hoc*
Est, or not at all. Inherences,
Or untenanted from *fiat lux*
For ever. The heart flutters, rises,
White as a petal bride, along aisles
Of moonlight... where's the groom?... she's seeking
His bloody cross beam to alight on,
But finds no thief bad or good, no Christ.

iv. 'the dark corners, the closed rooms'

He learned to be a Puritan in winter.
The plain parlor of the house where he grew up
In Salem, Massachusetts – outside, deep snow,
Within, a family by candle-light, and
Open on the table the prints of Flaxman,
Black on white, figures from Homer and Dante,
Sharp, suggestive templates which every viewer
Invests with hue and texture, tell their story.
The widow turns the pages and the children
Crane, question; they share the chaste stuttering light.
At the same time the boy takes something private,
Sensual to heart, so that when the fire's raked
Safe in the hearth, the candles snuffed and the house
Asleep, in his chamber, with the door bolted,
In the tumbled bed he lolls with her, and her,
Andromache or Dido, the Pleiades
Gracious, approaching, smelling of snow and stars.
He releases each heroine from her story,
Removes her robes and, clothing her with desire,
Banks night after night the furtive ecstasies
And the incremental guilt that Hester Prynne
Is the most artless and aberrant child of.
His darker thoughts are luminous. Like a cat,
He sees in the dark. Like a demon he watches
Darkness herself shake out her abundant hair.

'If ever I should have a biographer,
He ought to make great mention of this chamber.
So much of my lonely youth was wasted here,
Waiting patiently for the world to know me...'
It came to know him, he married happily.
He turned his haunting ancestors to fiction.

To his friend Bridge in 1850 he joked
How he'd finished his book 'yesterday; one end
Being in the press at Boston, the other
In my head here at Salem, so my story
Is at least fourteen miles long ...'
                                    American,
Abroad for years, he could not really explain
What it meant, or why he was 'always outside
Everything,' as Henry James said, an 'alien
Everywhere, an aesthetic solitary.'
The Marble Faun marked his last transformation,
But as before, he did not quite understand
What it meant to disclose, it might have been love.

Back at that Salem window, looking in now,
A December bird, he observes the widow,
Album, siblings – but the boy has disappeared.
Banished, or set free? Reluctantly he clings,
As if caught in bird lime, to the sill. 'There seem
Things I can almost get hold of, think about;
But when I am on the point of seizing them,
They start away, like slippery things.' He is snared
And plucked and seasoned. His language gropes, things and
Nothings. Too late he's come back home, all's altered.

Death of the Novel

At Preston Station Yevgeny Bazarov
Gave up the ghost. Having found his Russian heart,
A medical vocation, just starting out
For real, becoming good against his nature,
He died. My train was late again and the snow
Drifted across the platform. Closing the book,
I brushed the ice off of my cheeks, blew my nose.
I stamped my boots to get the circulation
Going, and so returned to the present tense.
Thomas Buddenbrook – at the height of summer,
Arriving at St Pancras, the evening light
In prisms playing on steel, slate and brickwork –
Clamped his rotting teeth. His heart stopped and he slumped
Beside me. I folded him away. I lost
Anna Karenina under the station
Clock in Baltimore. Speeding to Paris, Swann,
I abandoned you. The train had broken down
Just outside Turin when Gerald Crich arrived
At the hollow basin of snow, slipped, and fell,
'And as he fell something broke in his soul, and
Immediately he went to sleep.' I have lost
On trains, at stations, so many characters,
Don Quixote, Mrs Ramsay, Nepomuk
A mere child, Little Dombey counting the waves,
Nell, and Mesdames Bovary first and second,
Sweet Madame de Renal and her luminous
Glow worm. And worse, the very worst, Hurstwood, who,
Ragged and spent, in his small cold room, began
'To take off his clothes, but stopped first with his coat,
And tucked it along the crack under the door...

After a few moments, in which he reviewed
Nothing, but merely hesitated, he turned
The gas on again, but he applied no match.'

On his tombstone Norman Douglas had them carve,
Omnes eodem cogimur, we all reach
The same bourn. His final words, in character:
'Get these fucking nuns away from me.'
                                                    They die
Also, the authors, turning not into ghosts
Like ordinary pilgrims, but into stories
As real, if they wrote truly, as what they wrote.
Stevenson, for instance, still young when he died,
Is told and retold. Henry James adored him,
Man and boy, savouring him in his own words,
Reshaping him as his song, 'a child of air
That lingers in the garden there...' Samoa
Made him Tusitala, Teller. There he died,
Decanting a good bottle of Burgundy.
Omnes eodem. Conrad called on his friend
Stephen Crane at Dover. It was Crane's last day
In England. He lay in a hotel bedroom
'With a large window looking on to the sea.
He had been very ill and Mrs Crane was
Taking him to some place in Germany.
But one glance at that wasted face was enough
To tell me it was the most forlorn of hopes.'
Crane said, 'I am tired.' Then he said, 'Give my love
To your wife and child.' Looking back from the door,
'I saw he had turned his head on the pillow.'
Conrad watched from the threshold, noting how 'he
Was staring out of the window at the sails
Of a cutter yacht that glided slowly like

A dim shadow against the grey sky.' He pulled
The sea around him, tight around his shoulders.
It was cold.
    I stamp my boots. The train arrives.

After Hours

i.

And then, to tell the truth, I didn't much care.
I'd done my time and over. I wanted out.
Just as I was going they summoned me back.
The dumb thing is, I went. They offered money.
I had money enough; yet, when they added
You can keep your office and title, stupid,
I agreed. On short time I sit in the same
Chair at the same table, work piled before me;
Colleagues patronize me, I'm still Professor
Without professing, a spiderless cobweb,
While outside the sun climbs through the trees and time's
Not a clock but seasons, the kind an old man
Requires to make peace and walk into the woods
Like a pioneer, released from the routines
Of culture and employment. I didn't think
I cared, and then I stayed and the one who said
I've had enough walked away and wrote me off.

ii.

Good riddance, then. But I can't help wondering
Who he was, what he took with him, where he went.
I sit in the same chair at the work table
And think of him, not enviously. Did he go
To Cornwall where I thought I'd one day settle
In Fowey or Polruan, and walk the cliffs
At the end of England and the end of life
Loving the clouds and even the loud seagulls?
Did he go to Mexico and make a place,

Brief, perhaps, but radiant and very raw,
Having thrown his books and papers on the skip,
An Alp of literature, and chosen mountains,
Real mountains, the pine and cactus, coyotes
And gopher snakes, grey eagles, zopilotes,
And ocote smoke, pots of red rice, black beans
Hot on the brazier, at night so many stars
He found his place and gave up the glad ghost there...
Did he stay at home, his Alp of literature
Intact, wearing his Millet Myo Velcro
Climbing shoes, making his way with hiking poles,
Mammut Galaxy superdry climbing rope,
Crag-climbing gloves, crampons, ice-axes, ice-screws,
Leaving a sequence of huts and bivouacs
As he climbed the texts. Does he reach a summit?
And there in thin air does he find wings and rise?
Is heaven that way? To tell the truth, I care
For him, for all of him, cliff, star and summit.

iii.

His time is never up. I close my eyes, he's
There for sure, wearing my face, sun burned, wind burned,
He's written me off, so he never chides me.
I walk in his prints through the thick cliff edge grass
Or up the flinty cendero to the stars,
Or through deep snow and out across the ice fields.
My selves disown me but they remain my selves
Though my feet are dry, my hands clean, and I sit
In precisely the same chair at this table,
Fingering my Mammut Galaxy Super
-Dry climbing rope, wondering, will it take my weight?

III L'archéologie

Anacreon
After the Greek

i.

Again I love again I do not love
Am mad again and am not mad again.

ii.

I'm grey on the sides and white on top;
Youth that was nimble is gone, my teeth themselves
Ache and chatter, life's span is shortening, and I
Sigh more than sometimes, fearing Tartarus;
The dark forks of Hell hold terrors for me
And the pathway drops precipitate and once
A man starts down there's no way back.

iii.

Observe him, old Anacreon, frayed and worn, wobbly
With wine, how he bends his shape into the stone.
    He gazes, look at him, with eyes that look
    With love, with lust, and see too how his gown
Trails right down to his heel. In a haze of wine
He's lost one sandal, but the other still conceals
    A shriveled clutch of toes. The poet sings
    Of charming Bathyllus, full-fleshed Megistus
And he's strumming his melancholy lyre. O Muses,
Keep him safe, for it would be wrong indeed
    Were Bacchus' faithful servant to be felled
    By Bacchus' wine.

The Husband's Message
From the Old English

To you far away   I carry this message
I remain true   to the tree I was hacked from
Wood I am, bearing   the marks of a man
Letters and runes   the words of his heart
I come from afar   borne on salt currents
Hiss... in a hull I sought and I sought you
Where would I find you   my lord dispatched me
Over fathomless seas   I've come, here I am
Do you think of him still   my lord in your dear heart
Do you recall him   or is your mind bare
He remains true to you   true and with fixed desire
You try his faith   you'll find it stands firm

But hear me now, read   what is scratched on my surface

You, cherished treasure, dear   you in your youthful
Your hidden heart, dear   remember your vows
Your heart and his heart   when together you haunted
The lovely hamlets   the mead hall, the promise
To perform your love.
                    Well, all of that ended
In feud and in flight   he was forced from that place.
Now he has sent me   to ask you come to me
Cross the seas, come to me   come here with joy
When to your listening   on the steep hillside
First comes the cuckoo's voice   sad in the trees
Don't pause don't linger   come at that calling
Don't stay or delay   come at that call
Go down to the shore   set out to sea then
To the tern's chilly home   go south go south

Over the ragged sea   south find your lord
Come to him, there   he waits for you wedded
To your sure arrival   no other wish
But only the wish of you   You're more in his mind
Than Almighty God   whose power could bind you
One to the other   again as you were
Able to rule then   able to raise up
Your people, comrades   and endow you with jewels
Bracelets and carcanets   collars and combs
He has set aside for you   fair gold, bright gemstones
In a faraway land   among foreign folk
A handsome mansion   hectares and cattle
Faithful retainers
                        though when he set out
Pursued and a pauper   he pointed his prow
Out to the sea   alone set out sailing
Lost in his exile   yet eager to go
Weaving the currents   time in his veins

Now truly that man   has passed beyond pain
He has all he wants   has horses, has treasure
The great hall's warm welcome   gifts the earth yields
Princess, Princess   you too are his portion
Remember the promises   each of you vowed
The sealing silences   he made and you made
A letter, a syllable   nothing is lost
What seem erasures   are kisses and praying
Are runes that keep counsel   a promise in touch
A promise in looking   how staunch he has stayed to you
Above him the heavens   the earth under foot
A man of his word he is   true to your contract
The twining of wills   in those days gone in time

In this Modest Style

from the Spanish of Ramón López Velarde

It's how she spreads, without a sound, perfume
of orange blossom on the dark of me,
it's the way she shrouds in mourning black
her mother of pearl and ivory, the way
she wears the lace ruff at her throat, and how
she turns her face, quite voiceless, self-possessed,
because she takes the language straight to heart,
is thrifty with the words she speaks.

                                           It's how
She's so reticent yet welcoming
when she comes out to face my panegyrics,
the way she says my name
mocking and mimicking, makes fun,
but she knows that my unspoken drama
is really of the heart, though a little silly;
it's how, when night is deep and at its darkest,
we linger after dinner, indistinctly talking
and her laughing smile grows fainter and then drops
softly on the table cloth; it's her teasing, the way
she won't give me her arm and then allows
passion to chaperone us when we walk out,
when we promenade on the hot colonial boulevard...

Because of this, your whispered, modest style
of love, I worship you, my faithful star.
You like to cloud yourself in mourning,
And give, my hidden blossom; kindly,
Mellow, you have presided over
my thirty years with the self-effacing concentration

of a vase whose half-blown roses wreathe in scent
the headboard of a convalescent man;
                                        cautious nurse, shy
serving maid, dear friend who trembles
with the trembling of a child when you revise
the reading that we share; apprehensive, always timid
guest at the feast I give; my apprehensive ally,
humble dove that coos when it is morning
in a minor key, a key that's wholly yours.

I beatify you, modest, magnificent;
you have possessed the highest summit of my heart,
you who are at once the artist
of lowly and most lofty things, who bear in your hands
my life as if it was your work of art!

O star and orange blossom, may you go
lightly swayed in an unwedded peace,
and may you dwindle like a morning star
which the lightening greenness of a meadow darkens
or like a flower that finds transfiguration
on the blue west, as it might on a single bed.

September 1915

Quartet

From the Spanish of Octavio Paz

> *Ore, fermate il volo*
> *e, carolando intorno*
> *a l'alba mattutina*
> *ch'esce de la marina,*
> *l'umana vita ritardate e'l giorno.*
> — Tasso

i.

Known yet always strange, the lie of the land,
the riddle of the palm of one's own hand.
The ocean sculpts in each wave, stubbornly,
the monument in which it falls away.
Against the sea, a will that's turned to rock,
the faceless headland keeps the sea in check.
The clouds: they are inventing sudden bays
where a plane is a skiff that melts away.
The rapid scribbling of the birds above
others are fishing where the waters move.
Between the sea-foam and the sand I tread,
the sun is resting light upon my head:
between what's static and what will not stay
in me the elements enact their play.

ii.

There are tourists also on this strand,
death in a bikini, death with jewelled hand,
there are rumps and bellies, loins, lungs, thighs,

a cornucopia of bland enormities,
a scattered abundance that precedes
the meal of ashes where the worm will feed.
Adjacent, yet divided by those lines
strictly kept but tacit, undefined,
are vendors, and the stalls where fries are sold,
and panders, parasites, untouchables,
the rags of poor men and the poor man's bones.
The rich are stingy while the poor man fawns.
God loves them not, nor do they love themselves:
'each does but hate his neighbour as himself'.

iii.

The wind breaks forth and gathers up the grove,
the nations of cloud disperse above.
The real is fragile, wavering, unsure;
also, its law is change, it does not tire.
Round and round the wheel of seemings spins
upon a fixity: the axis time.
Light sketches all and then turns all to flame,
with daggers that are brands it stabs the main
and makes the world a pyre of mirrorings.
We are mere white horses of the sea.
It's not Plotinus's light, it's earthly light,
a light of here, but it is thoughtful light.
It brings, between me and my exile, peace:
my home this light, its shifting emptiness.

iv.

To wait for nightfall, I have stretched myself
under the shadow of a throbbing tree.
The tree is a woman in whose leaves
I hear the ocean roll beneath noon heat.
I eat her fruits that have the taste of time,
fruits of forgetfulness, fruits of wisdom.
Beneath the tree, the images and thoughts
and words regard each other, touch.
Through the body we return where we began,
spiral of stillness and of motion.
To taste, to know – it is finite, this pause:
it has beginning, end – is measureless.
Night enters and it rolls us in its wake;
the sea repeats its syllables, now black.

Anacreontea

After the Greek

i.

Beloved swallow, every year you come,
You weave a nest in Summer, then you're off,
Wintering near the Nile, at Memphis.
In my heart Eros, not regarding seasons,
Keeps weaving a nest, where one
Longing is fledgling, another still in egg,
A third just hatching; and the nest is loud
With wide-beaked chicks all clamouring for food.
The larger feed the baby Longings,
And when they are mature there in my heart
They themselves, in Eros' nest, begin begetting.
What am I to do, I am too old, too weak
To shout to silence this vast flock of Longings.

ii.

Anacreon, the Teian singer, in a dream
Saw and called to me. I ran and kissed him.
I hugged him. He was old but still quite handsome
And Love was working in him, the wine scented
His lips. Since he was old, unstable on his pins,
Eros clutched his hand and guided him.
The poet lifted from his brows the garland
And passed it to me, and it smelled of him.
I was a foolish boy, I placed it
On my own head as a crown, and ever since
I've not lived a single moment without love.

IV Surveiller et punir

Also, Poor Yorick

Yorick's heart is moved: how beautiful, he says,
And grasps then what it must mean to be human
Returning rested from the afterlife
Into the lovely dew of resurrection.
Bare feet, with the worms and roots still in them,
The puddles cool between their metatarsals.

The skulls bay with joy, and all are grinning,
Popping their knuckles, counting their vertebrae,
And now they dance alone and now join hands,
And as they dance there, in their ribs and rigging
In each grey skeleton a robin perches
Plumping its feathers, pulsing out its song

Red, and the twittering's blood as well as music.
– Never has he witnessed a scene so vital,
The dance of life the scripture guaranteed.
Faster as shadows shorten and noon rises
The skeletons spin and conga into the air
Making a cloud, a halo on the sun.

He takes his spade and sets it on his shoulder.
He's old. Till now he's known so much regret.
He's buried his grandparents and his parents,
His kings and queens, his brothers and his friends,
His lovers, all of them, consumables,
Pulvis, cinis, nihil, the bones bearing

In their chalk wholeness so much love and light.
In his own graveyard, with the dear departed
One unfamiliar skeleton stands up

Tall, gracious, folding down his finger bones
Over two holes; where his hurt feet strike stone,
Sparks from the rusty nails, and in his side

A spear, perch for a phoenix. Jesus Christ
Risen in this garden, and the wounds,
Or the bones that keep the marks of wounds, are singing.
It's noon, there are no shadows. This is true.
He raised them and himself is rising up.
Also, poor Yorick. That was judgement, it is over.

Later in the day the Prince arrives,
Stepping from his script as from a carriage
Drawn up among the holes in which the dead
Waited, and from which they are all delivered,
Just like an audience when the play is over
Elbowing their coats into the dark.

Anxious, a bit deranged, he finds occasion
To hold a conversation with a skull.
Is it a skull or a stone that looks like a skull?
The heads are all gone to heaven, Jesus too,
The sexton himself put off his flesh and followed.
(Ophelia was already on her star.)

Poor prince, alone with just a book of ballads,
With just the plot nothing can raise him from.

The Stove

*... and kisses on the rowan tree
the scarlet ulcers of the unseen Christ.*
Sergei Esenin, 'Autumn' (translated by Geoffrey Thurley)

In the big round stove they're burning up the trees.
It's hot all day in the tall kitchen. Outside
It's freezing, it's sunless as if a shadow was cast
By the ghosts of the trees that are burning, and the stove
Stays glowing all day, even when nobody's by.
They're burning the trees. All over mother Russia
The forests burn. Her face is grimed with soot.

They're not big trees but thin sticks of birch they're burning,
The graceful wings of pine and spruce, the blood-berried rowan.

Poem

23 March 2003

    i.

Mountains, rivers, waves of grain, red deserts, oceans!
Fifty stars, and not a single sun.

    ii.

Who writes the history? There is no war,
No victory or victor.
                        Separation, hearsay,
Gossip, innuendo, rumour
Whispered until there is a conjuration,
A demon spins into view and now
There has to be a war, and she the victim
Holds behind her back a scimitar,
Froth of blood still on it, and intones
How it has been, lays out the fresh wounds
Side by side like fish on a market slab.

The Wafer

'The Face of Christ', late fifteenth century, Dutch

Each takes a little, east and south and west,
Diminishes it, like nibbling the edge
Of a sweet biscuit, each takes a kiss of crust,
A lip of sugar, a lick of crumbs,
Each takes until remaining the blank core
Is mere erasure where His face had been.

On the Morning of Christ's Crucifixion

It wasn't at his birth the gods came down.
They didn't know the baby had arrived,
What he'd been, who he was, who he would be.
Olympus was home. For one more generation
They could meddle in the lives of us below,
Cross our true loves, plough our cities under
With war, raise storms, rattle the earth, and after
Return to the lowering clouds and sleep it off,
Starting again next day, as myth prescribed,
And so serve out eternities of mischief.

        Not all was mischief there. Mild Vesta swept
        Ash from a cloudy hearth, and Janus
        Sat on the stoop and watched another morning
        Climb the escarpments, molten, and the stars
        Dim, then drown like sparks in the rising light.
        The Larès were already at work in the barley fields,
        Pomona from the orchard brought a skirtful of blossom
        And Palès looked after goats in the upper pasture.
        Ops and Consus slept in the haystack till harvest.
        This is how it was, how it should have been.

Across a sea and in another language
A Roman and a Jew in quiet conversation

Under the wings of a cedar begin to change the world
Rock by fracturing rock, grass blade by blade.
They reach accommodation: Barabbas
Vanishes in the crowd, another captive
Is robed and crowned. He's king. He takes his cross
As men are made to dig out their own graves.
He falls and rises, is scourged, is cursed, is pitied,
He climbs to the summit assigned and is crucified.

Every mountain he has climbed, climbing that mountain.
Every mountain shaken. Rocks tumble down the sides.
Olympus too, where the gods have always lived,
Is beaten like a drum, the light explodes
And even here, as at Jerusalem
A crossbow with a man drawn taut upon it,
Drawn like an arrow aimed straight at the mid-day sun –
And suddenly the sun falls out of the sky.
It's as dark as just before the world was made,
As it will be when time at last is over.

The lights go up again. The crossbow on the summit
Is Christ drawn taut by his own gravity.
An altered sun burns over the whole earth.
Olympus feels it. The old gods are over.
The clouds have let them down. They blame a book
They never read before. They've been at sea: with a clang
Noah drops the enormous gangplank. The ark's grounded
Not on Ararat or Olympus. Golgotha.
Light is transfigured. The gods gather up their belongings.
They start down the broken path in dazzled pairs;

All stiff and molting, mangy with confinement,
Beasts out of the ark after months at sea,

Cawing, croaking, buzzing, growling they stumble.
They have forgotten where on earth they belong,
Seeing it afresh and frowning hard at it.
Now they are subject to the laws of kind.
The yellow rheumy-eyed lion with his glum
Mate is Jupiter. Where's their savanna?
Apollo, no longer brilliant, a wheeling eagle.
Diana bends at a pool and licks the light.

A dove who was Venus coos for her blank-eyed son,
Wherever he flew he's gone. There's lumbering Vulcan
Rutting, the boar he always was; and Mars, she says,
Where is Mars, will we ever again together
Swing in a single snare and be in love?
Mercury, already nesting, is a swallow,
Minerva, a blinking bay-owl, waits for nightfall.
Bacchus and Maia, he stumbling, she supporting,
Begin to bleat and whirr: goat, hummingbird.
After the privilege of Olympus, they are fallen.

Not all is altered there. Mild Vesta sweeps
Ashes from the cloudy hearth, and Janus
Sits on the stoop, watches another morning
Climb the escarpments, molten, and the stars
Dim, then drown like sparks in the rising light.
The Larès work in the barley fields, Pomona
Out of the orchard bears a skirtful of blossom.
Palès tends his goats in the upper pasture.
Ops and Consus wake. Is it harvest time?
This is how it is, how it should be.

Family Tree

Watching his creatures with a filial sorrow,
Christ, not a shepherd yet, not yet a man,
Propped on a cloud at the edge of things, his hands,
Unbroken, on his hips, wonders who he'll be
And knows it's up to Adam to determine
What human pleasure might feel like, and what pain,
To the son of God – Adam who's in mourning,
Adam whose Maker has withdrawn the Kingdom,
All for a fruit, a serpent and a rib.
The Son of God sees Eve grow plump as a pillow
Bearing a mallet and three nails inside her,
Bearing a spear, a sponge and vinegar.

A Carol for Edward Taylor

Long fields of yellow wheat
In Palestinian sun
Are ripening into flesh.
The vineyards on the hill
Bring forth a salty fruit.

There where the bread was torn
Off of the human loaf,
Where years began to count
Because a child was born
I come to eat my Word.

Before me at the rail
Is Stephen with the stones
Turned into loaves by love
And James of Zebedee
Carries his singing head;

Peter and Philip bear
Splinters of their cross trees,
Bartholomew his skin
Rolled up beneath his arm,
Thomas from India

With his appalling spear,
And sweet Sebastian too,
God's willing porcupine,
And Agatha whose heart
Is caroling with hurt,

Perpetua with her own new
Baby clutched at her breast,
Felicity her slave
Whose child will not be born
Attended by the beasts

That tore them limb from limb
And slouch now tame and meek
To Bethlehem, and kneel
The way the sheep and ox
Knelt on that first day.

Cyprian and Polycarp
Both try to sneak away
But drawn by the infant Host
Out-dazzling from his crib
The flare of martyrs' fires

(Antipas on the grill –
Domitian's brazen bull,
And all the melting saints
That lit his jubilees,
And later La Pucelle,

And in a northern town
Cranmer and Ridley too,
Transcendent kindling,
Making the tongues of flame
Speak so we understood)

They climb their Calvary
Carrying such precious gifts
As Africa can spare.
There where the wine was spilled
Out of the Virgin's womb

Belief and disbelief,
Faithful and faithless, kneel
Because, whatever's true,
A child is going to grow
On whom we can impress

Fear, hatred and desire,
A child we will impale
And plant in every grave.
We do it by the Book.
I come to eat my Word.